First published in the United Kingdom in 2014 by

St Giles
hospice

**St Giles Hospice,
Whittington,
Staffordshire,
WS14 9LH**

www.stgileshospice.com

Design cover and layout Dominic Pote

Edited by David Calcutt

With help from Glen Buglass, Rachel Parker and Dominic Pote

Layout and printing by HOLLYHILL DESIGN   www.hollyhilldesign.net

Being **Here**

This book is dedicated to all palliative care staff, hospice staff and volunteers who devote their time and skills to supporting the physical, emotional and spiritual care of patients and their families.

The publication date was timed to coincide with *'Dying Matters Week'* May 2014.

Being here opens a window
In my world,
Taking time out,
Watching and reflecting.

Being Here

This book is dedicated to all palliative care staff, hospice staff and volunteers who devote their time and skills to supporting the physical, emotional and spiritual care of patients and their families.

The publication date was timed to coincide with 'Dying Matters Week', May 2014.

Being here opens a window
In my world,
Joking time out
Watching and reflecting,

Contents

Being Here   An Introduction

This book is about people, the lives they have lived and are living and the memories and experiences that have made them what they are. It began as a series of writing and reminiscence sessions at St Giles Hospice. The aim of the sessions was to encourage those who both worked in and attended the Hospice; patients, nursing staff and volunteers, to share their life experiences, the people and places and things that mean something to them, those moments in time past that remain part of a vivid and ever-living present; their fears, their sorrows, their joys.

It seemed to me that the content of the sessions should not only provide the material for the written content of the book, but that it should be part of the same process of creative speaking and writing, should provide a simple but effective form through which those taking part felt free to speak in an open and intimate way. The written form I feel does this best is poetry. Poetry has a way of focussing attention on the small details of memory and experience and of bringing them up close, into the here and now, making them new and clear and fresh.

The method I used was a simple one. It was first of all to choose themes and subjects for talking about and writing about that were both general to everyone and yet particular to each individual, carrying with them some special significance and emotional charge. The sections in this book follow those themes. The writing was done on postcards, a few carefully chosen phrases by the writer, so that only the really important details were written down. Those images and feelings and sensations that were deeply embedded in memory and which, when written like this, in short lines, already began to look and sound like poems. These pieces were then used as the basis for discussion in small groups, which gave the people the chance to speak to each other in more detail about what they'd written, to share their memories and experiences.

These "postcard poems" have formed the basis for most of the content of this book. In some cases, the poems have been more or less as they were first written. Some I've worked on to a greater or lesser extent, moving words around, tightening up phrases. In poems written about specific places chosen by more than one writer, I have taken lines from them all and made them into a single poem. Other poems were made from notes taken from conversations with people. In one or two cases people wrote their thoughts out in prose and I took key phrases and made them into poems, hoping to capture the essence of what it was they had written.

But in all cases, no matter how little or how much I might have intervened in the originals, the words, the phrasing and the feelings expressed, are exactly those of the people who wrote or spoke them. Most importantly, it is their voices that speak from the pages of this book, sharing with us brief and intense moments of their lives, in the here and now, vivid marks made on the page and deep in the memory.

David Calcutt
Lead Artist

Foreword

St Giles Hospice provides high-quality specialist services that form an umbrella of care and support for people and families affected by life-limiting illness. I am sure you will agree that the many poems and images contained within this book provide a moving and inspiring testament to the thousands of people who are cared for by the hospice each year.

2013 was a special year for St Giles Hospice as we celebrated our 30th anniversary. It was also the year in which we invited artists into the hospice for our first Arts into Health Project. Through the writing and reminiscence sessions, it has been an honour and a privilege to be able to share the unique and precious memories of our patients. The project has also enabled us to commission beautiful and peaceful artworks to reflect those memories which will visually enrich our hospice buildings for years to come.

The word 'hospice' is derived from the Latin word 'hospes' meaning to host and welcome guests or strangers. This description of our purpose - 'to host and welcome guests and strangers' - is further emphasised by our name 'St Giles' as St Gilles (the French spelling) was an eighth century hermit in the south of France who offered hospitality to pilgrims. Above all, I feel a hospice is a place where people can come together, to care and support one another, with compassion, friendship and love. To quote just one of the poems within this book, St Giles Hospice is where you will find, 'People connecting … With a strength of shared emotions, Relaxed with new friends and strangers', a place where 'everyone is so caring' and you will be given 'warmth, friendship and support, … the richness of people'.

I wish to convey my sincere thanks to all the patients, family members, artists, staff members, carers, volunteers, funders and supporters for their contribution to our Arts into Health Project and for making this book and the accompanying artworks possible.

Peter

Peter Holliday
Group Chief Executive

Being **Here**

The Happiness of Stories

Is like a big family gathering,
Relaxed and informal,
Meeting people, hearing laughter,
Socialising, feeling happy.

Hearing stories brings back memories.
It's lovely to recall fond thoughts,
The happiness of shared stories,
The comfort, the friendship, the help.

It's a sanctuary where I forget my woes,
And I am just glad to be alive,
Where people are unfolding
And all is well.

Unique **Memories**

Unique **Memories**

A Group Poem

Happiness
A Group Poem

Birth of my daughter
Giving me hope
Green fields, stillness, peacefulness.

Sitting on top of the Long Mynd as the sun rises,
A chill in the air, but warmth in my heart,
Sunshine and warmth with a quiet sense of freedom,
A splash of golden orange, carefreeness and ease.

Conversation with friends,
The warmth, the happiness,
Wine and laughter.

Seeing my father smile,
Calm and content,
My hand on his face.

It was worth the effort.

Birth

The Calf Being **Born**

Waiting patiently
In homely comfort,
Unaware, excited
With fear, anticipation,
Kindness, compassion,
Understanding and care
And trust.

And then
A unique explosion
Of joy and pain.
Oh, my God, it's coming!
It's a boy!
Hear him cry.

The cow looked in pain.
I stroked her head and spoke to her,
Then I saw the calf's head
And the calf itself, being born.
It struggled to stand at first,
But the mother leaned down
And licked its head,
The cow showing
Her love for the calf.

Moving Up

I was born and grew up in Nechells.
They were back-to-back houses
With no garden and no kitchen
And where you shared an outdoor toilet.
To us it was normal.
It was the olden times.

When I was sixteen
They knocked the street down
And rebuilt the place, they built flats.
We moved to Ward End,
We had a house with a kitchen
And a garden.

Bloody Nora!
A garden!
We'd moved up a stage.

First Walk with a Grandchild

First Walk with a Grandchild

Just the two of us.

The smile she gave me,

The love and the trust,

The feeling of her being part of me.

That small hand reaching up to take mine

As we took our first walk together.

Falling Backwards

Falling Backwards

Laughing

Into the bright green bracken,

Sweet-smelling, curly fronds,

Spiky stalks, blue sky above,

Holding hands with my big sister.

Hoylake

Hoylake

A fishing village on the Wirral
Not far from Liverpool
That's home for me,
Born and bred.

My grandfather was a fisherman
We used to queue up on the quay
Waiting for them to return
With their fresh catch

And play on the beach,
Collecting pop bottles
Left behind by the tourists,
Getting money back on them from the shop.

On an island not far off shore
There's a bird sanctuary
And I've seen dolphins from there
You can walk across when the tide's out

And my brother got stuck there
Once at high tide
And had to wait for the tide
To go out again.

Watching Swans

On a bright and fresh autumn morning,
Standing with my friend, feeling preoccupied.
Then the swans flew down and landed on the river,
And I remember the sound and the scene before me,
My thoughts and senses coming back
To the beauty of that moment, and to the company
Of special friends.

Falling In Love

Boyfriend and girlfriend in a field,
A warm summer night,
Watching shooting stars,
Falling in love,
A feeling of foreverness.

Full Circle

Full Circle

I was living in Birmingham with my husband
He didn't talk to me, not about anything
I thought, Is he even listening?
Something was missing. What was it? Me.
So I got up one morning
I got up from the bed where I lay with my husband
And just went walking
I was gone a long time.

There was this guy, my lover,
He was a Muslim, I'm a Sikh
I was born a Sikh, in the Punjab
We met and we just went
The bus, the train
We rented places, we were together
He made me laugh all the time.

We were in Bradford and he drank a lot
He was always drunk, I said he should stop
In the end I had to leave him.

I came back
My sister-in-law helped me
I've been everywhere
Birmingham to everywhere
And back to Birmingham
I've been full circle.

Moving at a **Slower Pace**
Moving at a Slower Pace

I had holidays on the canals.
There were about six or eight of us.
You go through all those towns,
And you don't know where you are,
You might be anywhere.
They've got their own little wildlife,
The countryside within the town,
And you're oblivious,
You're in your bubble,
Your own little world,
Moving at a slower pace.

Bank **Vole**
Bank Vole

We were in a car park
And I saw a bank vole eating
A blade of grass.
Its teeth were working overtime.
It didn't seem to notice us,
It looked so warm and furry,
I could see its heart beating.

A **Stroke** Maybe

A Stroke Maybe

I may have had a stroke,
I'm not sure.
I know I went dizzy
And I kept falling over.

The ambulance came, I said:
"I don't want to go to hospital"
But the medic said that I should go,
If I'd had a stroke then I should go.

They did a scan on my brain
They did an E.C.G.
They put these clamps
On the sides of my head
And put this thing over my face.

And it was like a hammer
Inside my head,
Fifteen minutes,
Bang Bang Bang.
It seemed like forever,
A hammer in my head.

Then the nurse took it off,
She said I'd been good,
But it wasn't nice,
It wasn't nice at all.

And they're still not sure
If it was a stroke,
It might have been my MS,
It might have been a stroke,
And they're still not sure.

Diving

Diving

An amazing explosion of colour and life.

Underwater rainbow of coral sculpture

Shaped like fingers, leaves and brains,

Shafts of sunlight like krypton splinters

Capture myriad shoals of technicolour fish

But beware the crown of thorns!

An Ever-Present **Mystery**

An Ever-Present Mystery

Trust and support,
Soft, unfaltering light,
Beauty in the mystery
Of the magical presence.
Silence in the connection of everything,
An ever-present guiding mystery.

Good **Memories**

Good Memories

Smell of cut grass,
Lovely walks in the woods
When all the bluebells were out.
Good memories.

A Group Poem

A Feeling of Foreverness
A Group Poem

The front door slamming, followed by silence.
Dark, chocolate brown paint on the walls,
Eyes open, complete blackness,
The smell of apples.

Family trips, happy, complete,
My brother up the tree,
Bank vole eating a blade of grass,
Cheeky little apple-thief!

Coiled, patterned danger in rustling reeds,
Torrents of water over the lock-gates,
Mask, air, water, surface,

An amazing explosion of colour and life.

Very frosty, cold day, brilliant sunshine,
Sketching views with the smell of cut grass,
Falling backwards, holding hands,
Crushing bracken, laughter.

Music, family, friends,
Watching shooting stars
In love and comfort and happiness.
The small hand reaching up, the trust.

A feeling of foreverness.

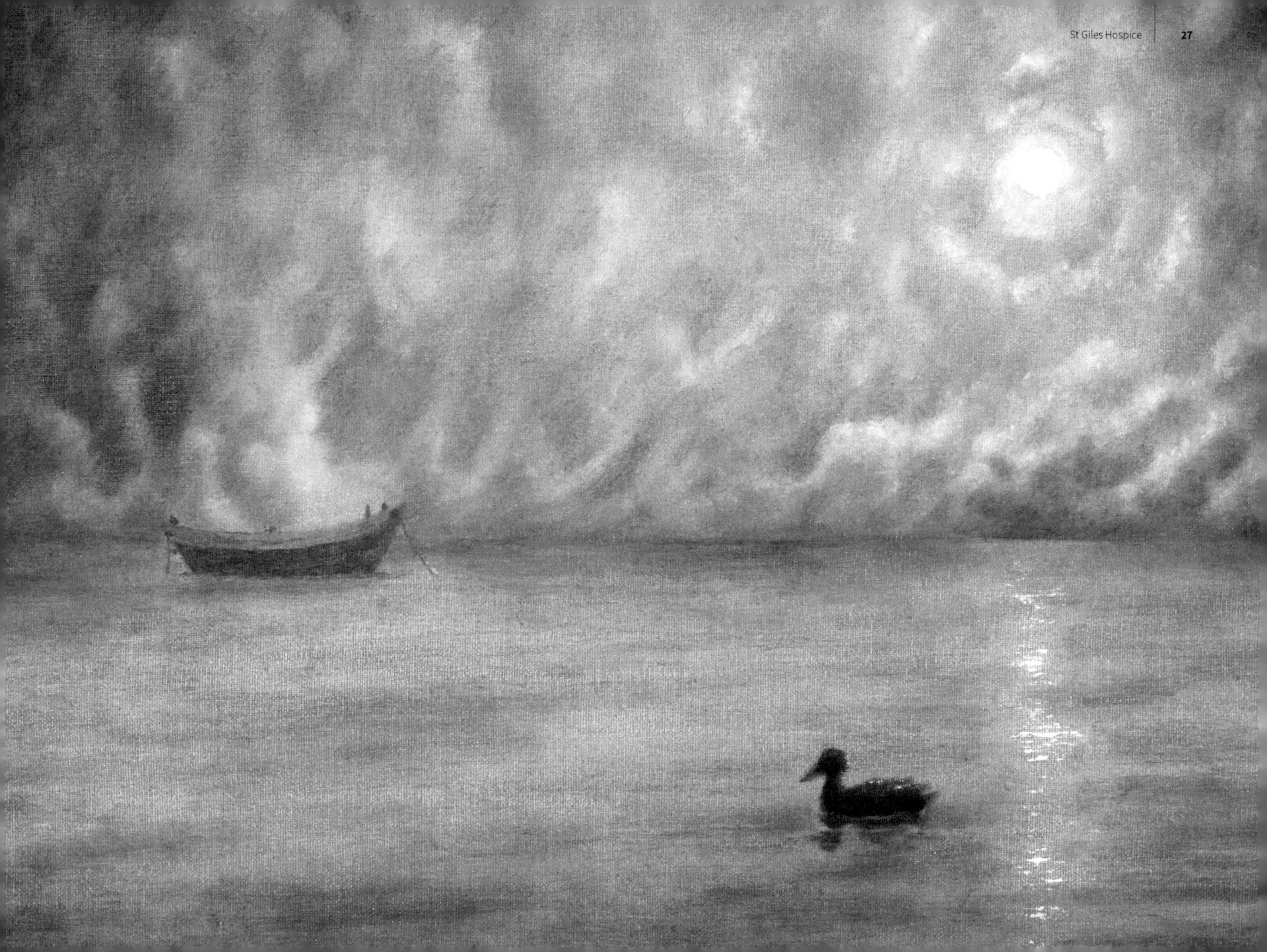

Meaningful Places

Meaningful Places

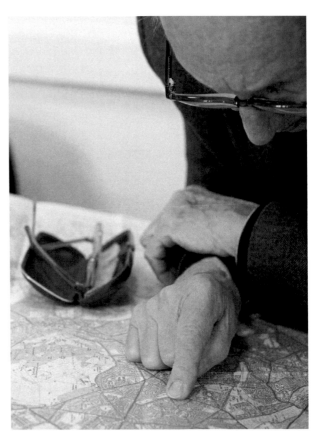

My Grandparent's House

Where I was born.

The attic room,

Sloping roof and low ceiling.

Eyes wide open,

Lying in the darkness

But not afraid.

Drifting back to sleep

And the room drenched

With the smell of apples.

Kingsbury Water Park

Where Sandra ran after her son,
Happy, exhilarated,
Riding his bike
For the first time,
As the children laughed
And the dogs barked.

Branston Water Park

Blue water trickles
Birds sing
And Stephen took a walk
Around the lake
Feeling calmness in nature's way.

Lathkill Dale
Lathkill Dale

In Derbyshire,

Where water comes fresh and clear

Out of the ground,

Trickling over rocks,

Bounded by green trees.

Unconstrained, at one with nature,

Barbara tried to catch a fish,

And Pam's husband proposed.

Canwell Ford
Canwell Ford

Trees, water, bikes.

Racing down the hill

With the rest of the boys,

Faster and faster

Down into the shallow stream,

Splashing through the ford at Canwell.

The joy of speed

And getting wet.

Formby Point

Boats and ships passing

From the Mersey to the sea.

Hazel scattered her mother's ashes there

Beneath the hopeful, Beatle-blue

Of the Liverpool skyline.

Fradley Junction

Fradley Junction

Where you hear the creaking

Of the locks opening and closing

And the water is calm

And Nina threw a ball

And her dog jumped in.

Tamworth Castle

Tamworth Castle

Where the two rivers meet,

Trees seem to have their own personalities,

Fairytale images, a concealed magic,

And Belinda feels the flow of the place

In the glistening reflections

Of light on the water.

New House

New House

Cold concrete slabs in the pantry,

Dark chocolate brown paint on the walls,

Noisy bare floorboards.

Green-patterned linoleum,

Worn and tired,

Musty, damp, dusty, dark and exciting.

Who lived in this house?

Kingstanding

Kingstanding

The mound and the trees,

Autumnal russets,

Swirling, dancing circles.

Gazing into the past,

Pondering, finding the answer.

Loneliness.

Lichfield Cathedral Close

Lichfield Cathedral Close

Looking up at the worn faces looking down

From the deep sandstone blocks,

Listening to the children walking and chattering,

Joanne made her pilgrimage

Towards peace and happiness.

The Border Cottage

A cottage on the Welsh border,
One beautiful Spring weekend

And memories of an old man.

There were lambs
And there were bulbs springing up.

I felt exhilarated.

I don't know why it means so much,
But it always comes back to me.

Snowdonia

Mike went fishing
In clear water,
Caught a fish,
Felt peaceful.

Castleton

Castleton

In the Peak District,
Where Jayne climbed hills
That go on forever,
Escaping from the fast pace of life,
Feeling calm, and weightless.

On Scafell Pike

On Scafell Pike

Up on Scafell Pike
A rowan tree saved my life.
Scree fell away
Hundreds of feet below,
So I hooked my arms
Round that tree
And Sheila was saved
And so was I.

Hopwas Woods

Hopwas Woods

Where the sun streaming through the trees

In the cold winter

Brings peace and quiet

And gives Nicki time to think.

Ludlow

Ludlow

Where Viv worried

About remembering her lines,

Hearing the sheep bleating,

The birds singing,

Watching bats flying

Around the castle at night.

Rhudlan Castle

Rhudlan Castle

In North Wales,

With its space ruin view through the window,

Where Margaret watched her child falling

And the sky was blue

And the birds were singing

And her child was safe.

My Garden

Neglected, out of control.

I had other things to do,
My family in a time of crisis.
I wanted it to be as it was.

Now I'm finding it again,
Piece by piece
It's changing for the better.

Maybe it happened for a good reason,
Because it's making me happy again.

Cannock Chase

Cannock Chase

A mass of colours,

Green to orange to brown,

Where Colin spent his early courtship days,

And, in the stillness of a sunset,

A herd of deer

Cross in front of Barbara's car.

Sutton Park

Sutton Park

Golden leaves on the ash trees
The rustling of leaves in the autumn breeze
Birdsong on a sunny, fresh day.

Valerie rides her bike through the trees,
In the peace and quiet
Feeling free.

Sue smells the wood stove
In the café
Thinking about how things change.

Becky walks hand in hand with her boyfriend
Talking, laughing
Feeling happiness in friendship

And in love.

Langdale

I was in a coma for three weeks.

As I was coming round
I was hearing everyone around me
But I had no way of letting them know
That I could hear them.

I tried to stop my head from wandering,
I made myself focus on one place,
One word: Langdale.

It's a log cabin near Ullswater.
We have a timeshare there,
It's so quiet, so peaceful,
The best time of the year.

And so I said: Langdale
Again and again and again
To come back to my husband.

Bracebridge Pool

Bracebridge Pool

Bridges large and small,
Trees swaying very tall.

Water lilies white and green,
Woodpecker never seen.

Calmness from summer's glow,
Cold feet and hands – will it snow?

St. George's Wood, Yoxall

St. George's Wood. Yoxall

Broken heart tree

In the golden buttercup pasture,

Close by the stream

And the badger sett,

Hearing a buzzard call overhead,

Looking back at my home below.

Significant People

Significant People

My Daughters

My Daughters

It was a cloudy day

In spring

The day

We adopted our daughters.

I was apprehensive,

Happy and relieved

The day

We became

A real family.

Dad

Dad

Roast dinners were his speciality

And those Bermuda chats

That went on forever.

I was amazed he never learned to swim.

The key figure in our family,

He ruled with a rod of iron.

Now he's gone, and I'm free.

It feels strange.

My Father

My Father

My father drank.
When I was born he didn't want me.
I was eleven years old
When he died of drink.
It was the first time I ever felt safe.
I didn't have to look over
My shoulder anymore.

After he died
I saw him in my bedroom,
He was standing there,
Looking straight at me.
It happened again.
I asked him what he wanted.
"Better late than never," he said,
And that was the last time I saw him.

Two Friends

Two Friends

I lost my friend, Audrey, who died.
I lost the sound of her voice,
I lost her smile,
The advice she gave me,
The touch of her hand.

And yet…

I found my friend, Wendy,
In the Day Hospice.
We share our problems,
Her smile lights up her face
When she sees me…

And my heart sings.

My Baby Daughter

My Baby Daughter

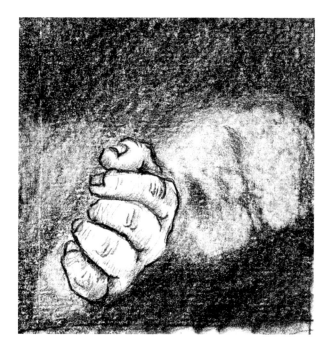

A warm sunny day,
Holding my newborn baby daughter.
She was the second
And she was dark haired.

A cold sunny day,
Holding my baby daughter's coffin.
She was the second
And she was dark haired.

Others have come after,
I appreciate them,
But she's in my mind
All the time.

I saw her on that Saturday afternoon

And as soon as I saw her

I knew she was mine.

But I didn't know how to get her.

So I just said to her,

"What would you say

If I said I love you?"

She said, "That's nice."

And that's what started it off.

Sheila

Soul Mate and Special Friends

Soul Mate and Special Friends

My soul mate was someone
Who understood me.
Now my feelings are empty,
I feel incomplete.
It happened without explanation.

But these special friends
Are filling that gap,
Not replacing, but helping me
Along this roller-coaster journey

Wishing someday to land
In a happy place
Where me and my soul mate
Will be reunited.

Life

I lost my father
Because of cancer.
I felt he'd been taken
For the saving of me.
Then I had my first cancer.

But three cancers later
I'm a stronger person,
I appreciate life more,
My family mean much more to me,
Other things are not so important.

All the money in the world
Will not buy me my health.

Precious Things

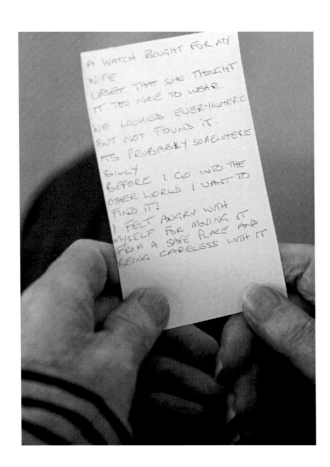

A WATCH BOUGHT FOR MY
WIFE.
UPSET THAT SHE THOUGHT
IT TOO NICE TO WEAR.
WE LOOKED EVERYWHERE
BUT NOT FOUND IT.
ITS PROBABLY SOMEWHERE
SILLY
BEFORE I GO INTO THE
OTHER WORLD I WANT TO
FIND IT!
I FELT ANGRY WITH
MYSELF FOR MOVING IT
FROM A SAFE PLACE AND
BEING CARELESS WITH IT

Precious Things

A Group Poem

Precious Collection
A Group Poem

A Buddha from my brother
A timepiece from beyond time
A photograph of family memories
A gold cross from my parents
A 21st birthday bracelet
An embroidery of an owl
A Queen Victoria Jubilee mug
A wooden box of paper hearts
A brooch from a beautiful lady
A pipe smoked by my great-granddad
A clock with the family name on the dial
An opal ring from my special sister
A brooch, the last thing my mother gave me
A piece of lava from an extinct volcano
Dad's DIY tools, the right tools for the job
A key chain for friendship
A jar filled with memories
A book of meanings.

A Key Chain for Friendship

A Key Chain for Friendship

In the shape of a turtle shell,
It feels lightweight,
Holds friendship
From a long distance away,
In Mexico,
The last time I saw my friend.

A Flower Brooch

A Flower Brooch

One rose, many memories.

Beautiful colours, heavy to the touch,
But warm, because it's from my mother.
She gave it to me before she died.
I keep it in a box in my bedroom
And she's there at night with me,
Looking over me,
She's with me all the time.

It looks beautiful against a black dress.

Gold Cross

Gold Cross

You remember the outstanding things,
But the little things you forget.

This gold cross,
I always wear it around my neck.
It's part of me, it is me,
It gives me comfort,
Reminds me of my faith,
My parents' love.

It's lonely within,
But I feel God is always with me
In my lonely little world.

Opal **Ring**

Opal Ring

A present from my twin sister.
The stone changes colour in the light.
It's comforting to wear.

It was given to me on our special day,
A lively night out
To celebrate our eighteenth birthday.

Happy, loving memories,
A special time that will never be again.
I always feel complete when I'm wearing it.

Brooch from a Beautiful Lady

A mouse with a tail of silver stones,

Small, light.

I wear it on my yellow jacket

In memory of my mother

And spring in the countryside

Where I was born.

An Owl To Greet All Callers

Embroidered tapestry,
Feathery and soft,
My creation of beauty
For posterity.

For some reason I'm drawn to it,
Perhaps all the hours spent
Of happiness and love.

Now it stands in the hall
To greet all callers.

The Little Box

The Little Box

Smooth and light to the touch,

A little box of cedar wood,

Given by my sister.

I keep it in my bedroom

And the smell transports me

Back to Bermuda.

Bracelet

Bracelet

Silver, gold,
Engraved, inlaid,
Solid and weighty,
Cool and beautiful.

I remember wearing it for the first time
On my twenty-first birthday in 1952.
Now I've given it my granddaughter,
A lasting love.

I said, *"Wear it as and when."*
She said, *"Thank you, grandma, I will."*

I'd like it to become a family heirloom,
But people who come after
Won't know what it was to us.

Mug

Mug

I bought from an antique shop

In a little town in Wales.

Now it rests on a wall unit

In my sitting room

And I think about

What it was like back then,

In the days of Queen Victoria's

Diamond Jubilee.

Jar

Jar

From Sicily,

A two-handled water-jar

Sits on my window-sill.

It was my granddad's,

Warm and comfortable

With childhood memories,

The pilgrimage we made,

Leaving for England.

Lava

Lava

Jeep safari experience in my bedside cabinet.

To hold a piece of lava from an extinct volcano.

We went into the core, I picked up this piece,

Heavy, hard and rough, with a green stone

And a memory in the middle.

An Ivory Pipe

An Ivory Pipe

It was kept on the mantelpiece at home,
Small, smooth, nut-handled,
Carved with a horse and a dog.

My father treasured it.
I was told not to touch it
For fear of damage.

It belonged to my great-grandfather
And his teeth-marks are on the stem.
And in the bowl still
A plug of un-smoked tobacco.

The Family Clock

The Family Clock

Stands on the shelf in the sitting room

In its heavy mahogany case

With our name on the dial.

I remember it striking

In my mother-in-law's house.

Now it reminds me of my husband.

Lovely to look at,

Handed down through the family,

It will be passed on.

The Right **Tools**

The Right Tools

They were my dad's and his dad's
From ages gone by,
Old and well-worn.

I keep them clean every time they're used,
Keep them tidy and clean.

The old tool is the best tool for the job.

The love and the memories in the shed.
What's going to happen to them when I'm gone?

Painted **Hearts**

Painted Hearts

A wooden box filled with painted paper hearts,
A Valentine's Day gift from my boyfriend.

He cut out each one and painted them red,
Sealed them in a letter and sent it to me

With a letter that read, *"I love you."*
I keep it on a shelf in my bedroom,

The wooden box filled with painted paper hearts
And love.

Lost and **Found**

Lost and **Found**

A Group Poem

Time Passes
A Group Poem

Sometimes I open the door and there are shadows,

Empty feelings,

Great sadness.

A terrier dog,

A gold ring,

An old coin,

A box that disappeared.

We looked and couldn't find it,

It meant the world to me,

It cannot be replaced.

Lost in war,

She was wearing a little white dress,

Taken for the saving of me,

All the money in the world will not buy me my health.

How could I explain?

My inability to do things for myself,

Maybe it happened for a good reason.

Time passes,

The memory lingers on,

My heart sings.

A Watch for My Wife

A Watch for My Wife

I bought a watch for my wife.
She thought it too nice to wear.
I was upset, I moved it
And now it's lost
And I'm angry with myself
For being so careless,
Moving it from its safe place.

Since my brain tumour was removed
I've grown impatient,
I can't do things for myself, I'm frustrated.
I look out of the window
And watch my wife cutting the grass.
I think, *"I should be doing that."*

I want to find that watch
Before I go to the other world.

Lost in War

Clock

A man lost in war,

Amongst his belongings

A ruby ring.

A photograph of four brothers,

One of them wearing

A ruby ring.

Could this be my father?

A 1930's clock

From the other side of the world.

My mother saw it and thought of me,

Carefully brought it back,

Presented it with pride for my new home.

Vanished.

Careless.

Sorry, Mum.

Cat

Cat

Who found who?

A black and white face at the window,
A silent miaow
Sending me feline thoughts.

Now, snugly, softly,
Cosied up to me each evening.
She found me

And a home.

Engagement **Ring I**

The stone has fallen out twice
And twice it's been found,
Once in the bedclothes,
Once at the bottom of the stairs.

I've had cancer twice
And I'm still here.
I promised to be here
For our Golden Wedding.

I think I'm lucky.
It reminds me
That we're here
For a purpose.

Engagement **Ring II**

A ring is a never-ending circle,
My ring is very near to my heart,
The diamond has been lost
Yet twice has been found,
I hope it will never more depart.

Two rings are worn on my finger,
Two rings symbolic of our love,
I'll keep them forever
While I'm here on this earth
And perhaps when at last go above.

Lost for Years

Lost for Years

The necklace was lost for years
And when I found it again in my handbag,
I felt such relief and joy

But the photo of my daughter,
Six months old before she died
And wearing a little white dress,

I put that in the envelope
With the other photographs
And when I looked for it again
It was gone.

The necklace meant so much to me.
She had the most beautiful smile.

My Father's **Medals**

My Father's Medals

His World War medals.

My mother gave them to me

Before she passed away.

I kept them in a tin box

In the garage,

But the box disappeared

And all the memories I had.

A Harmonious **House**

A Harmonious House

A sorrow felt,

Not afraid,
Not angry or scared.

There are memorable dreams.

Sometimes I open the door
And there are shadows,
But I'm not frightened.

We have a harmonious house.

Time

Time is past

But I do not consider it gone.

Time passes,

Time gone,

Regained, re-lived.

They are not lost memories.

Being **Here**

A Window in my World
A Group Poem

A Group Poem

Peaceful and calm,
Caring, friendly,
Away from the familiar four walls.

Being here opens a window
In my world,
Taking time out,
Watching and reflecting.

The tranquillity quietens the soul.

It's a paradox,
An overwhelming experience,
So glad I came.

In my last moments,
When I give my last gasp,
I hope I am here.

A Building Like No Other

A Building Like No Other

It stands alone
In an oasis of farmland,
Unpretentious,
A red brick building
With few windows.
The magic begins as I enter.

People are not coming here to die.
They're sharing an opportunity to live
And this is what binds us,
A dominant heart
Of interior warmth.

The gift of life
Is a gift to be shared.

From outside it's a building
That's like no other.
Inside it shares its life force
With all who cross the threshold.

The **Final Poem**

the final poem

I

Listening to stories,
Precious memories shared,
Humbled, barriers down,
Sharing nervous giggles,
Watching others smile,
People laughing, feeling good.

II

Everyone's deep in concentration and thought,
People connecting
With a strength of shared emotions,
Relaxed with new friends and strangers,
Giving time, finding peaceful thoughts,
A little piece of our innermost feelings.

III

Help! I can't do it!
But everyone is so caring, and sharing,
I love seeing the faces all around,
Their reluctance and shyness,
Surprise and pleasure,
Their commitment and enduring enjoyment,
Warmth, friendship and support,
Smiles exchanged, the richness of people.
Happy at the outcome, I laughed out loud,
Surprised I could do it after all.

IV

Privileged to be part of something special,
Everyone on the same level,
Being in the same place, on the same road,
Life as a common person
Finding happiness in someone else's story
And learning from each other
The way others view the end,
An animated face, a calm life.

V

Creativity is uplifting,
It gives people a way of life,
Confidence to talk,
Pride and passion,
The happiness of different ideas.
I feel uplifted by the power of creativity,
The warmth of people's poems,
It gives an insight into what can be done,
Into my own mortality
And the courage of the human condition.
Searching for thoughts,
I gave my own precious memories.

VI

Settled and content,
Calm, our tasks completed,
With a deep sense of satisfaction and achievement,
I was happy to take part
And make a difference.

*Becky Wright is a nurse at
St Giles Hospice in Whittington
and took part in the project.*

*After the final session she was moved
and inspired to write this poem.*

What is **Hospice Care?**

What is Hospice Care?

It's the pushing together of two beds
In the softly lit room of a couple
Enabling them to hold each other
In the silence of the night.

It's helping the man to buy a special gold locket
For his wife for Christmas
As he knew he would not be there
To give it her himself.

It's running with the child
Who has fled his mother's room
When she died and holding him in silence
As his world pours out in uncontrollable sobs.

It's the Nurse's gentle touch of reassurance that

'I AM HERE FOR YOU
RIGHT NOW
I AM YOURS TO LISTEN'.

Of course there are tears
But there is also much laughter,
Strange as that may be
And yes there is Symptom Control,
Support and Guidance

But, it's the little tiny actions that we give
That is Hospice care to me.

The Artists

Peter Tinkler

Shortlisted for the Young Artist of the Year Award, 2011 Newcastle, Peter has obtained degrees in both Illustration and Animation and a scholarship in Layout Drawing and Storyboarding from Colaiste Dhulaigh, Dublin. Recent exhibitions of his work include *Word is Drawn*, London, *Addiction*, Birmingham, and *The Biscuit Factory Foundation*, Newcastle. Concepts of narrative are important in his work - paintings are not merely arbitrary fragments of time confined by the boundaries of the canvas, but unwinding stories that invite the viewer to question what is being represented.

Peter is influenced by many artists, but also classical literature, and of course the greatest stories of all - our myths and folklores. He delivers regular art workshops for both adults and children. He was born in the Rep. of Ireland.

David Calcutt

David is a playwright, poet and novelist. He has written many plays for professional and community theatre groups, and for BBC radio, and his poetry has appeared widely in magazines. His novels include *Crowboy* and *Shadow Bringer* for Oxford University Press and *Robin Hood* for Barefoot Books. His most recent publication is *Through The Woods*, a book of narrative poems and paintings, created in collaboration with fellow poet Nadia Kingsley and artist Peter Tinkler, published by Fair Acre Press. David's latest theatre work includes *"Journeys"*, a piece written and directed for the Stratford Literary Festival, based on stories collected from residents of care homes, and a one-man play, *"The Life and Times of the Tat Man"*, which is touring between May and December 2014.

Dominic Pote

Dominic Pote is a fine-art photographer with over 12 years experience of making unique photographic artworks to commission with a particular focus on healthcare projects. His large-scale landscape artworks, rooted in community consultation and workshops, bring the positive restorative quality of nature into the healing environment. Without the aid of a digital camera or other technological devises, Dominic creates images that suggest the actual experience of time. Hazy and dreamlike his photographs imitate the process of memory itself. Working somewhere between the film-maker and the still photographer his exposures last as long as he keeps moving. Dominic has twice received Arts Council awards for the development of his work and has been commissioned and collected by organizations such as the British Council and Barclays Bank. UK Healthcare commissioners include The Gloucester Royal Hospital, The Queen Elizabeth Hospital Birmingham and Palliative Care Centre, Walsall.

Ming de Nasty

Ming has been working as a self employed photographer for 25 years. She started her career by taking photos of bands and musicians. She has produced photographic images for companies, museums, art galleries and councils across the country. As well as many solo photographic exhibitions she has had photographic works in exhibitions around Britain and in Europe. She also runs workshops in photography, digital photography and Photoshop skills.

The Creative Development **Team**

Glen Buglass

Glen Buglass is manager of Walsall Council's Creative Development Team. Glen specializes in arts project management, creative thinking and organisational development and works with public and private sectors. His background is in performing and he worked as an actor, guitarist and teacher before joining Walsall Council's Creative Development Team in 1994. He co-edited the well received community arts handbook, *'Making Choices, Finding Voices'* (Educational Heretics Press, Nottingham).

Rachel Parker

Rachel Parker is Principal Arts and Health Officer for Walsall Council's Creative Development Team. She is passionate about arts and health work. Rachel enjoys managing a diverse range of arts projects and finding innovative ways of using creativity to promote people's health and wellbeing. Rachel studied Theatre Design and worked in the theatre before she joined the team in 2000.

The Artists and the Project

Dominic Pote

For me, spending time at St Giles has been a positive, inspiring experience. I have witnessed a caring supportive community and feel honoured to have engaged, in a small way, in the life of the hospice. Through the creative workshops I have been involved in the sharing of memories and the unfolding of lives; a creative, therapeutic process in which people share both joys and sorrows and come together in a unifying sharing and celebrating of life.

For all of us memories are very important and especially as we get older and reflect upon our lives. Listening to people talking about their memories I have noticed how memories are often interwoven with intensely visual recollections of specific places. At the core of our positive memories there are particular landscapes. We can clearly remember the season, the weather, the colours and the smells attached to a memory. It is these places and their associated memories that I hope to capture through my work.

People at the hospice have shared their memories of places with me and I have been out to visit those places with my camera (at least those that were not too far away) and tried to capture them, striving to create not just a photograph, but an impression, a landscape work that embraces the living memory. I hope that the photographs presented here in this book pay homage to all participants' memories whilst at the same time offering to others positive landscapes that evoke calm and contemplation. Some of the pieces here have been made into large artworks for the walls of the hospice and hopefully will bring a sense of the landscape into the building, especially for those who may no longer be able to venture out into the landscape.

Peter Tinkler

The St Giles Hospice project was a huge challenge. The idea of being responsible for transforming peoples' life experiences and memories, through their own words, into one-off illustrations was a daunting task. But such challenges often force you to grow, improve, and even innovate. Before the first session I wasn't sure what to expect, but I remember being glad that I was working with people who had a lot of experience. I quickly realised that the group at St Giles were brimming with enthusiasm for an opportunity to discuss various aspects of their lives. Their positive energy and overall eagerness to share their stories was infectious, and lent the sessions a genuine vitality that exceeded my expectations.

I decided early on that the poems about their favourite places I would render as oil paintings onto canvas, whilst a selection of all the other topics I would render as black and white graphite and charcoal drawings. The choice in contrasting techniques was a very deliberate one. I felt the 'places' illustrations needed the effect of colour and light to carry the mood and atmosphere of the words describing them. To render them in black and white would diminish the splendour inherent in special places of nature. I had the idea of using limited colour schemes to capture not only something of the landscapes themselves, but also to use it as a metaphor for the landscapes contained within the human condition. Only colour could possibly come close to capturing even a semblance of this idea.

In contrast, it seemed wholly appropriate to render the other images as loose, graphite and charcoal drawings. Our memories can often have that hazy, dream-like quality about them, so I felt charcoal would capture that non detailed look most effectively. The paintings were well planned, with a very definite approach to the lighting, whereas the drawings afforded me the opportunity to 'loosen up' and not worry myself with complicated detail. It is tempting to go into more detail about the images I have created for this book, but I think its probably best to let them stand as they are, perhaps only to be properly judged by the people who inspired them.

What I would say is that these illustrations are simply my interpretation of their words, and my images cannot possibly hope to contend with their memories. But my hope is that they add something of value to the overall atmosphere of nostalgia surrounding the project.

Ming de Nasty

I was commissioned to do documentary photography during the creative writing sessions at Whittington and Sutton Coldfield St Giles Hospice. During the first session I chose not to take any photos and to take part to give me time to get to know the participants. I think it is important to know the people you are trying to photograph and to begin to build relationships with them and nurture trust. Throughout the sessions everyone was warm and caring, the room was full of people deep in thought.

The majority of the pictures I took are portrait based. I tried to concentrate on the individuals that were taking part and show their enthusiasm and sharing. I tried to capture their happiness and enjoyment, to contradict the perception of a hospice. I wanted the viewer to see the participants in that space where they are lost in their own creativity.

Acknowledgements

A project like this doesn't happen on its own. Thanks goes to everyone listed below who has contributed their valuable time, creativity, support and enthusiasm.

Nikki Archer, Beryl Arnold, Edith Ayres, H Ballanski-Chx, Vivian Barnes, Colin Barron, Norma Bellamy, Alan Blount, Pauline Bogue, Sue Bond, Glen Buglass, David Calcutt, Susan Charles, Brenda Chick, Mary Clarke, Jean Colley, John Daniels, Rowan Davies, Ming de Nasty, Hayley Downes, Anna Eddleston, Diane Edwards, Margaret Forde, Jenny Francis, Joanne Gardner, Dennis Gibbons, Barbara Gibbons, Steven Gilbert, Vickie Gilbert, Mandy Glover, Arthur Graham, Sue Guest, Pam Handscombe, Margaret Hinks, Peter Holliday, Nicki Holmes, Elaine Horton, Walter Howard, Tez Hynes, Sandra Ingram, Nina Jackson, Roberta Jarvis, Wendy Jones, Fran Jones, Clara Jones, Wendy Jones, Lesley Jones, Lee-Michael Langmaid, Joan Latham, Ian Leech, Mike Lewis, Sue Matthews, Richard Morris, Julie Nicholas, Janet Ogden, Belinda Owen, Rachel Parker, Joyce Parker, Stella Pass, Shirley Phillips, Gordon Pidgeon, Pauline Pinner, Dominic Pote, Karen Puzey, Susan Richards, Sarah Riches, Karen Roberts, Avril Seabridge, Lyn Shiel, Peter Simm, June Smith, Barbara Stanley, Lesley Stinton, Peter Tinkler, Jayne Tooth, Barbara Wallin, Janet Webb, Joy Weetman, Rosemary Weston, David Willday, Colin Williams, Joan Wilson, Adrian Woodward, Becky Wright.

The St Giles Hospice Arts into Health Project was funded with the support of the Garfield Weston Foundation, the Albert Hunt Trust, the Lord Austin Trust and the Staffordshire County Council Community Arts Fund.

Quotes from patients and staff

Quotes from patients and staff

'Excited and privileged- To be part of something so special'

'There has been care and support for each other - a deeper understanding and a strength of shared emotions'

'Warmth of the people's poems - Happiness of being involved'

'When I came in today I was so glad to see all the people as I hadn't been out all week'

'Exhilaration because everybody was eager to participate - Surprise that so much has been achieved -
A deep sense of satisfaction and achievement'

'Delight at the bringing together of such different people and sharing creativity is uplifting'

'Warmth all around- Relaxed with new friends and strangers'

'Really lovely to hear the noise of people chatting and laughing in the room'

'Coming here on a Tuesday helps me realise and remember that I am not alone.
It's a lesson to be thankful for what we have- there is friendship and support here!'

'Whilst we were working together in the sessions, I forgot I had cancer'

'You made it seem so easy when you were working with us. It was like we had done nothing –
no writing as such. Now we have a book!'

Quotes from patients and staff

Quotes from patients and staff

'Excited and privileged - To be part of something so special.'

'There has been care and support for each other - a deeper understanding and a strength of shared emotions.'

'Warmth of the people's poems - Happiness of being involved.'

'When I came in today I was so glad to see all the people as I hadn't been out all week.'

'Exhilaration because everybody was eager to participate - Surprise that so much has been achieved - A deep sense of satisfaction and achievement.'

'Delight at the bringing together of such different people and sharing creativity is uplifting.'

'Warmth all around - Relaxed with new friends and strangers.'

'Really lovely to hear the noise of people chatting and laughing in the room.'

'Coming here on a Tuesday helps me realise and remember that I am not alone.
It's a lesson to be thankful for what we have - there is friendship and support here.'

'Whilst we were working together in the sessions, I forgot I had cancer.'

'You made it seem so easy when you were working with us. It was like we had done nothing –
no writing as such. Now we have a book.'